W9-CWK-236

Kindness

Marcia & David Kaplan
art by Danny Patterson

The material in this book has been compiled over a long period of time. Many of the sources are unknown to the compilers. We wish to acknowledge the original authors whoever they may be.

This book is dedicated to —
Special people who
make happiness happen
through their kindness.

Kindness –
It's a hard thing to
give away because it
usually comes back!

Blessed are those who give without remembering and take without forgetting.

...Elizabeth Bibesco

All doors open
to courtesy.

...Thomas Fuller

*Anger improves
nothing
except the arch
of a cat's back.*

…Coleman Cox

*Write your sorrows
in dust
and your blessings
in granite.*

*Learn to enjoy
little things —
There are
so many of them.*

Some people are like good watches.
They're pure gold,
open-faced,
always on time,
dependable,
quietly busy
and full of good works.

Those who think the competitive spirit is dead ought to watch the customers in a supermarket when a cashier opens a new checkout lane.

...James Alexander Thom

Patience!
The windmill never strays
in search of the wind.

        ...*Andy J. Sklivis*

*The only people
with whom you should
try to get even
are those who have
helped you.*

...Mae Maloo

Do more than belong,
participate.
Do more than care,
help.
Do more than believe,
practice.
Do more than be fair,
be kind.
Do more than forgive,
forget.
Do more than dream,
work.

...William Arthur Ward

Happiness is a habit –
cultivate it.

...Elbert Hubbard

*Better keep yourself
clean and bright;
You are the window
through which
you must see
the world.*

...George Bernard Shaw

*A kind word warms
for three winters.*

Chinese Proverb

*The ladder of life
has splinters,
but they ALWAYS
prick the hardest
when we're sliding
down.*

...William L. Brownell

Appearances are
deceiving –
the dollar bill looks
exactly as it did
a generation ago.

Snowflakes offer a lesson on the value of teamwork.

No two are alike, but they cooperate on jobs they couldn't possibly handle alone – like tying up traffic.

*Every act
of kindness done
makes life nicer
for someone.*

*We can't all be
shining examples,*

*but we can at least
twinkle a little.*

Things worth remembering:
  The value of time.
  The success of perseverance.
  The dignity of simplicity.
  The worth of character.
  The virtue of patience.
  The wisdom of economy.
  The power of kindness.

There is no tranquilizer in the world more effective than a few kind words.

...*Pearl Bailey*

*All the beautiful
sentiments in the world
weigh less than a
single kind action.*

*Everyone has a fair
turn to be as great as
he pleases.*

...*Jeremy Collier*

*A cloudy day
is no match
for a sunny disposition.*

The optimist sees the doughnut, the pessimist, the hole.

...McLanburgh Wilson

*What lies behind us
or before us
are small matters
compared to what lies
within us.*

...Ralph Waldo Emerson

When you get a good idea, act as if you're sitting on a tack. Jump up and do something!

Aim high! It is no harder to shoot the feathers off an eagle than to shoot the fur off a skunk.

...Troy Moore

Every survival kit should include a sense of humor.

God gives us faces;
we create our own
expressions.

Why is it that winter freezes your hands and feet, but thaws your nose?

A brook would lose
its song
if God removed
the rocks.

*Make the most
of all that comes
and the least
of all that goes.*

You cannot climb up hill by thinking downhill thoughts.

Things to give thanks for:
Your family,
your home,
your job,
your health,
your country,
your freedom,
your intelligence,
your curiosity,
your optimism,
your sense of humor.

People who can bounce back from setbacks will always be front runners.

*The control center
of your life
is your attitude.*

*Joy is not in things,
it is in us.*

Life is a succession of lessons which must be lived to be understood.

...*Ralph Waldo Emerson*

Don't get too big for your britches; you're sure to be exposed in the end.

Politeness is
to human nature
what warmth is
to wax.

The way to have a better tomorrow is to start working on it today.

Don't be discouraged; it's often the last key in the bunch that opens the lock.

High octane happiness is a blend of gratitude, service, friendship and contentment.

*Most of today's worries
are like puddles –
tomorrow they will
have evaporated.*

Public speaking is like taking a vacation. It helps to know the right place to stop.

*Good health and
good sense are two of
life's greatest blessings.*

The man on the top of the mountain didn't fall there.

Enthusiasm is the match which lights the candle of achievement.

And remember,
we all stumble,
every one of us.
That's why it's a comfort
to go hand-in-hand.

...E.K. Brough

The best way to cheer yourself up is to cheer everybody else up.

...Mark Twain

*In life
pain is inevitable,
but misery is
optional.*

We must always have
old memories
and young hopes.

…*Arsene Houssaye*

*We all live under
the same sky,
but we don't all have
the same horizon.*

*Life's blows cause
some men to wail on;
And others to sail on.*

*It's not the load
that breaks you down;
it's the way you carry it.*

Laugh a little – love a little
As you go your way!
Work a little – play a little,
Do this every day!

Give a little – take a little,
Never mind a frown –
Make your smile a welcome thing
All around the town!

Laugh a little – love a little
Skies are always blue!
Every cloud has silver linings –
But it's up to you!

...Phillips

*It's not your
age that matters.
It's how your
matter ages.*

FINANCE REPORT

Goodness is
the only investment
that never fails.

...Henry David Thoreau

A laugh
is a smile
that bursts.

...Mary H. Waldrip

*If fate throws a knife at you,
there are two ways of
catching it —
by the blade or
by the handle.*

...*Oriental Proverb*

*This is
the perfect season
to be the salt
of the earth.*

*The surest way
to make a red light turn green
is to try to find something
in the glove compartment.*

...Gary Doney

Ideas are very much like children –

Your own are wonderful.

*Continual cheerfulness
is a sign of wisdom.*

*When you become
reluctant to change,
remind yourself of
the beauty of autumn.*

*The peak years of
mental activity are
between the ages of
four and eighteen.*

*At four
we know all the questions.*

*At eighteen
we know all the answers.*

The important thing about your lot in life is whether you use it for building or parking.

*Play is for adults;
for children it's
serious business.*

The only chance
most people get
to start at the top
is in digging a hole.

Talent, like muscle, grows through exercise.

The darkest hour is only 60 minutes long.

Even when adversity has the bases loaded, the optimist expects to make a triple play.

*A candle loses nothing
of its light
by lighting another
candle.*

...Kelly

When you're flat on your back there is no way to look but up.

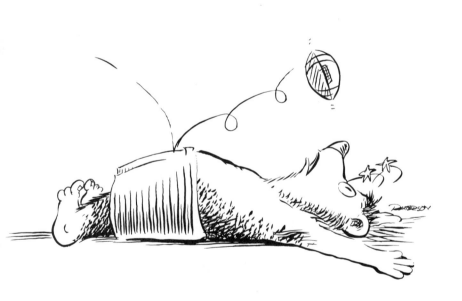

*Our days are like
identical suitcases —
all the same size,
but some people can
pack more into them
than others.*

Every life has its dark and cheerful hours.

Your level of happiness comes from choosing which to remember.

It's the little things that matter most.
What good is a bathtub without a plug?

*No man fails
who does his best.*

...*Orison Swett Marden*

*Remember the whale –
when it is spouting,
it is most likely to be
harpooned.*

*If you can give
your son or daughter
only one gift,
let it be enthusiasm.*

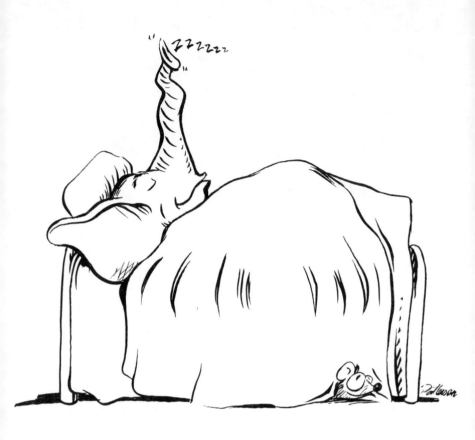

*No matter how big
or soft or warm
your bed is,
you still have to
get out of it.*

...Grace Slick

'Tis the set of the sails
and not the gales
which decides
the way to go.

...Ella Wheeler Wilcox

Pull Together!
You can't row a boat
in two directions
at the same time.

Always bear in mind that your own resolution to succeed is more important than any one thing.

...Abraham Lincoln

*Time flies;
but remember you are
the navigator.*

*Wishing you
new awakenings,
treasured memories,
and all the happiness
your heart can hold!*